Shakespeare's
F l o w e r s

Shakespeare's
Flowers

Introduction by Frances Owens

FRIEDMAN/FAIRFAX
PUBLISHERS

*I*ntroduction

"Away before me to sweet beds of flowers."

These words, with which Orsino retires to dream of love at the end of the first scene
of William Shakespeare's *Twelfth Night,* could just as aptly serve as our invitation to step into
an Elizabethan world of gardens and orchards, woods and meadows, flowers, herbs, and
common weeds.

Among English writers, few have been as knowledgeable of plant lore or as deft
with plant imagery as William Shakespeare. In Shakespeare's plays, nearly thirty scenes—
comic, romantic, tragic, and historic—unfold against a garden backdrop. The yellow-gartered
Malvolio marches ridiculously up and down the garden to the amusement of Sir Toby Belch,
Sir Andrew Aguecheek, and Maria, who watch from their hiding place in a box tree. Love-
smitten Romeo leaps over the high wall into Juliet's garden, where the nightingale sings in a
pomegranate tree. The ghost of Hamlet's father recounts how he was murdered with a
poisonous herb as he slept beneath his fruit trees. In the ancient garden of London's Inner
Temple, representatives of the houses of Lancaster and York pluck red and white roses and
set England on course for a bloody war that will send, as the Earl of Warwick prophesies,
"a thousand souls to death and deadly night."

A remarkable number of plants—more than one hundred fifty—appear in Shakespeare's
works. Unlike other poets of his era who employed stiff, stylized allusions to a standard set of
flowers, Shakespeare writes with familiar, even affectionate, knowledge about ordinary plants.
He calls them by their folk names, describes them with vividness and freshness, and sometimes
sounds as if he knew the pains of gardening firsthand. His metaphor for England suffering
under the yoke of Richard II is an image that would alarm any gardener:

> *... the whole land,*
>
> *Is full of weeds, her fairest flowers choked up,*
>
> *Her fruit trees all unpruned, her hedges ruined,*
>
> *Her knots disordered, and her wholesome herbs*
>
> *Swarming with caterpillars.*

Was Shakespeare a gardener? Probably not. Wealthy gentlemen like William Shakespeare did not dirty their own hands in the garden but employed teams of gardeners to set out plants, trim the topiaries, and clip the borders in their knot gardens. Shakespeare, like generations of Englishmen before him, loved plants and gardens, and he lived in an age when the passion for gardens reached a peak as a result of social, economic, and even religious factors.

Renaissance scholars, rediscovering ancient Greek and Roman works in botany, began translating them into English in the sixteenth century. Works that had previously been available only in manuscript form could now be widely distributed thanks to the printing press. In herbals, or plant encyclopedias, readers could see an illustration of a plant, learn how to grow it or where and when to gather it, and read about its many "virtues" or uses. Books like Thomas Hill's *The Profitable Art of Gardening* and Thomas Tusser's *Five Hundred Points of Good Husbandry* instructed readers in the arts of pruning and grafting, listed the gardener's monthly chores, and suggested garden designs, including intricate patterns for knot gardens like those Shakespeare describes as "em'rald tufts, flowers purple, blue and white/Like sapphire, pearl and rich embroidery."

The Protestant Reformation also influenced English gardening practices. Huguenots fleeing persecution in the Low Countries took refuge in Protestant England, where they introduced new varieties of flowers, new methods of cultivation, and new designs for gardens. Vast tracts of land, acquired by Henry VIII when he dissolved the monasteries, were being shaped into elaborate and extravagant pleasure gardens attached to great country houses. England's exploration of the New World further stimulated the interest in plants; far from home, English sea captains collected exotic specimens for botanists to study and for wealthy clients to display in their gardens.

Shakespeare lived in London—the center of England's Renaissance fervor—for about two decades. During several of those years he lived on Mugwell Street, not far from one of the most famous herbalists of the time, John Gerard, who maintained a garden containing one thousand different species. Shakespeare, like his audience, must have been familiar with Gerard's *Herball* of 1597, one of the most popular plant books published in the Elizabethan era, and it is likely that he was acquainted with the herbalist himself.

The transformation of herbs, or "simples," into medicinal compounds was certainly a familiar experience to Londoners. Professional apothecaries plied their trade in an area called Bucklersbury; so copious were the sweet odors produced there by the distillation of herbs that the neighborhood was supposedly immune from the plague. Falstaff alludes to this fragrant corner of London when he derides perfumed courtiers as "lisping hawthorn buds, that come like women in men's apparel, and smell like Bucklersbury in simple-time."

As important as all these factors may have been, Shakespeare's childhood in the country-side of Warwickshire did far more to shape his acute awareness of the natural world. Growing up in Stratford-upon-Avon, surrounded by a lush green world, the young Will Shakespeare must have absorbed plant lore as part of the everyday rhythm of rural life. Plants grew on the riverbank, in the farm fields, in dense hedgerows, and in the woods outside town, as well as in countless gardens. Outside modest homes, colorful drifts of flowers bloomed in informal cottage gardens. "Pot herbs"—what we would call vegetables—filled housewives' kitchen gardens. Physic gardens—perhaps no more than a corner of the garden plot—provided medicinal herbs. The most dramatic gardens were the precisely patterned, formal gardens that graced houses like Kenilworth Castle, within walking distance of Stratford.

Gardens were a source of delight and pleasure, but they were also essential in the management of a household, as the Queen in *Cymbeline* describes:

> ... Hast thou not learn'd me how
> To make perfumes? distil? preserve? Yea, so
> That our great king himself doth woo me oft
> For my confections.

Shakespeare would have watched the women in his life transform plants into household cleaners, cosmetics, and medicines. From their still-rooms emerged beauty waters, sweet bags, pomanders, and a wide variety of medicinal syrups, tinctures, oils, and cordials like the one King Edward uses as a metaphor:

> A pleasing cordial, princely Buckingham,
> Is this vow unto my sickly heart.

Herbs, as almost all green plants were commonly known in Elizabethan times, were vitally important in any sixteenth-century household. Rushes gathered from the river's edge were soaked in tallow and burned as "rush-candles." They were thatched into roofs, the "eaves of reeds" mentioned in *The Tempest*. They were spread as a covering on hard, cold floors ("Is supper ready, the house trimmed, rushes strewed, cobwebs swept?" demands Grumio in *The Taming of the Shrew*). The poor, like the jailer's daughter in *All's Well That Ends Well*, even fashioned pieces of rush into makeshift rings ("Rings she made/Of rushes that grew by and to 'em spoke/ The prettiest posies").

Other plants, particularly aromatic ones, helped make sixteenth-century life easier and more pleasant. Ladies held tussie-mussies of herbs and flowers to their noses when they braved the nauseating odors of city streets. Herbs strewn among the rushes on the floor, as well as spread on windowsills and burned in special perfuming pans, masked foul smells in rooms. Even royal palaces faced this problem; Queen Elizabeth's staff included a rose-petal-strewer and a royal herb strewer who had six assistants. Lavender and rosemary, laid in clothes presses, protected woolen garments from moth damage. Concoctions of deadly plants like hellebore banished vermin such as flies, lice, and bedbugs. With a handful of lemon balm from her garden, a housewife could polish and perfume her wooden furniture as Anne Page directs the elves to do in *The Merry Wives of Windsor* : "The several chairs of order look you scour/With juice of balm and every precious flower."

Elizabethan women also turned to their gardens and fields for ingredients to make cosmetics. The ashes of burned rosemary wood were used to clean teeth, while sage cooked in wine or beer was swished through the mouth to whiten teeth and fix the holes. Particularly prized were "those fresh morning drops upon the rose," dew collected from roses before dawn, which was distilled into beauty water that promised to clarify the complexion. Women used ivy berries or chamomile to change the color of their hair, they attacked dandruff with oil of rue, and they brushed their hair with wormwood in chicken fat to kill lice and make the hair grow thick.

Most importantly, the Elizabethan housewife depended on plants to protect her family from disease. Relying on recipes handed down in manuscript books or in printed herbals, she treated everything from simple problems (hangover cured with ivy steeped in wine) to life-threatening ones (broken bones in the head mended with a plaster of vervain, rue, and betony).

Some of the remedies were efficacious. Dr. John Hall, Shakespeare's son-in-law, became famous for curing scurvy with a compound of brooklime, watercress, marigold flowers, rosemary, and saffron. Herbalists often prescribed oil of thyme for chest complaints and coughs; today's cough remedies still contain thyme derivatives.

Other treatments were more dubious. The most common prophylactic measure against plague was the consumption of a fig, a walnut, and three sprigs of rue each morning. This probably caused a violent purging or even a terrible allergic reaction to the irritants in the rue, but plague was such a constant and horrifying threat that people resorted to draconian measures to avoid contracting it. Shakespeare, who lived through several outbreaks of plague in London, was, no doubt, well-versed in various preventatives, and he may have been paraphrasing the advice in a 1578 treatise on the plague when he has Margaret command, in *Much*

Ado About Nothing, "Get you some of this distilled *carduus benedictus,* and lay it to your heart. It is the only thing for a qualm." Thomas Brasbridge's *Poore Man's Jewell* recommended laying holy thistle *(Carduus benedictus)* "to your heart," promising that it will expel the poisons that "hurt and annoy it."

The highly superstitious Elizabethans recognized that what the friar in *Romeo and Juliet* calls "the powerful grace that lies in herbs" extended beyond such practical uses. In a world where supernatural beings, sometimes evil ones, lurked just beyond man's ken, plants offered a daring insight into, and protection from, a mysterious realm.

Shakespeare places Titania, queen of the fairies, on a "bank where the wild thyme blows" because, according to folk custom, fairies are drawn to thyme and sleep in its tiny blossoms. Daring Londoners bought a thyme unguent that was supposed to give them the power to see fairies. Those who preferred to court ghosts could acquire second sight by carrying a branch of lavender. Countless love rituals revolved around plants. Young girls placed a leaf of ivy beneath their pillows to inspire dreams of their future husbands. Once they were married, they ensured their spouse's fidelity by tying three bay leaves to the bedstead or by tapping his finger with a sprig of rosemary.

The typical sixteenth-century playgoer watching *Macbeth* unfold on the stage at the Globe would have been genuinely frightened by the Weird Sisters but took comfort in knowing that the powers of evil could be repelled or reversed by the judicious use of herbs. Householders, for instance, relied on the power of holly to draw lightning away from the house and to protect its inhabitants from witches. Planting hellebore nearby, they believed, prevented evil spirits from crossing a threshold; in fact, so powerful was hellebore's magic that country folk gathered it on Midsummer's Eve and hung it in stable and home to protect animal and human from bewitchment throughout the year to come. Elder leaves draped over windows and doors counteracted witch-craft. A hedge of rue, blooming with flowers as yellow as the sun, stopped witches in their tracks.

In the four centuries since Shakespeare presented his plays on the stage, we have lost much of the folk knowledge and superstition about plants that was second nature to his audi-ence. Beyond the simple lyricism of images we understand—the lover as "my sweet rose," a woman "as pure/ As the unsullied lily," lovers entwined in each other's arms "as doth the woodbine"—subtle meanings of the text or customs that have faded from memory elude us.

Ophelia's farewell speech, for example, might seem to modern readers merely the ravings of an unstable mind. The sixteenth-century audience, however, would have recognized it as a pointed message to the people Ophelia addresses. Each flower and herb that Ophelia distributes symbolized a vice or virtue, and this connection was immediately clear. Did the audience gasp when Ophelia gave columbines, whose pointed petals represented the horns of cuckoldry, to the queen? Nod in agreement when she presented the queen with rue, symbol of regret and repentance, and the king with fennel, symbol of falseness and flattery? Weep when she gave her brother rosemary, the symbol of remembrance and a clear reference to her own impending death?

The garland Ophelia wears in death is also significant. Garlands of sweet herbs and flowers, the "virgin crants" that Laertes insists his sister be allowed, were traditionally carried before the coffin of a maiden and then hung on the walls of the church in her memory. Ophelia, however, has woven a garland of wild flowers and weeds that symbolize the circumstances of her short life: crowflowers represent her maiden state; nettles, pain; daisies, love spurned; long purples, the chill of death.

Another of Shakespeare's tragic characters, King Lear, also dons a chaplet of plants in his final mad days. Lear's choices of weeds and wildflowers, which he has gathered on the heath, are ironic when we consider the theme of blindness—literal and figurative—in the play. Fumitory was reputed to restore clear sight, hemlock to cure disorders of the eye, and darnel to cause blindness.

Oberon's use of a flower charm to make Titania fall in love with the first thing she sees when she awakens—an ass—seems to us merely an amusing fancy. Shakespeare's audience not only believed it could happen, they recognized the very flower Puck uses, "Love-in-idleness," as Cupid's flower or heartsease, which we now call Johnny-jump-up. The flower had a long association with love dating back to the Celts, who brewed it into a love potion. No doubt more than one gentleman in the Globe audience was being treated for venereal disease with a syrup made from that same sweet plant, as sixteenth-century herbalists recommended.

Darker uses of plants also lurk in Shakespeare's lines. The witches in *Macbeth* conjure up visions with a brew of ghastly ingredients, including plants traditionally linked to witchcraft. Country folk believed that witches gathered hemlock, a poisonous meadow plant, after dusk because plants collected in the dark were more potent. Indeed, the hemlock used by the Weird Sisters has been "digged i' th' dark." The yew that they have "Slivered in the moon's eclipse" was associated with funerals since classical times. Yews line the graveyard in *Romeo and Juliet*, and the clown in *Twelfth Night* sings, "My shroud of white, stuck all with yew/O! prepare it!" Two other items in the witches' cauldron, called by their somewhat misleading country names of "adder's fork" and "tongue of dog," are also plants. The first is wild geranium or Robin-in-the-hedge, one of many notorious poisons used by witches to cast spells. Tongue of dog is the fern *Cynoglossum officinale*, whose seed, like that of all ferns, was used by witches to make themselves invisible.

Shakespeare's tragedies frequently hint at traditions linking plants to funeral rites. Violets appear many times in Shakespeare's verse, where they are praised for their delicacy, sweet scent, and intense color. Symbols of youth and spring, they nonetheless carry a tinge of sadness. Their ephemeral bloom so early in the year makes them a natural symbol for a life cut short. "I would

give you some violets," mourns Ophelia, "but they withered all when my father died."
Before long, Ophelia herself will be dead, and her brother will declare, "Lay her i' th' earth/And
from her fair and unpolluted flesh/May violets spring," a reminder of the ancient Roman custom
of planting violets on a virgin's grave.

Rosemary, a symbol of remembrance since ancient Greek times, was widely used at
funerals. When Juliet is discovered apparently dead on her wedding day, Friar Lawrence directs
her family to "stick your rosemary/On this fair corse; and, as the custom is/In all her best array,
bear her to church." Rosemary, however, was also a symbol of fidelity, and as such, figured
prominently at weddings. Brides wore garlands of the herb, attendants carried sprays of it, and
guests were given gilded sprigs of rosemary tied with colored ribbons as mementos of the occasion.
Juliet's father gives voice to this bitter twist of fate, declaring:

All things that we ordained festival
Turn from their office to black funeral
Our bridal flowers serve for a buried corse
And all things change them to the contrary.

When William Shakespeare retired to Stratford, he did not stop writing. Settled once more
in the rich green countryside of his youth, he finished several plays, including *The Winter's Tale*.
Completed about five years before Shakespeare's death, this play fairly bursts with allusions to
flowers, herbs, and gardens. Did the poet find inspiration for his vivid images in his "curious-
knotted garden?" Did he muse on the inexorable passing of the seasons as he trod paths of
chamomile, remembering the old proverb he had put in Falstaff's mouth: "For though the
camomile, the more it is trodden on, the faster it grows, so youth, the more it is wasted, the
sooner it wears"? Brushing against strong-scented rosemary, did he wonder how he would be
remembered in ages to come?

For you there's rosemary and rue; these keep
Seeming and savour all the winter long,
Grace and remembrance be to you both.

Could he have imagined that one of his simplest descriptions of a garden seems a
metaphor for the treasures he left us?

This garden has a world of pleasures in 't.

Yet marked I where the bolt of Cupid fell.

It fell upon a little western flower,

Before, milk-white, now purple with love's wound,

And maidens call it "love-in-idleness."

A Midsummer Night's Dream

There's fennel for you, and columbines.

There's rue for you, and here's some for me;

we may call it herb of grace o'Sundays.

You must wear your rue with a difference.

Hamlet

Our bodies are our gardens, to the which our wills are gardeners; so that if we will plant nettles, or sow lettuce, set hyssop and weed up thyme, supply it with one gender of herbs, or distract it with many, either to have it sterile with idleness, or manured with industry, why, the power and corrigible authority of this lies in our wills.

Othello

. . . daffodils,

That come before the swallow dares, and take

The winds of March with beauty . . .

The Winter's Tale

. . . though it do work as strong

As aconitum or rash gunpowder . . .

Henry IV Part II

. . . Not poppy, nor mandragora,

Nor all the drowsy syrups of the world

Shall ever medicine thee to that sweet sleep

Which thou owedst yesterday.

Othello

So doth the woodbine the sweet honeysuckle

Gently entwist; the female ivy so

Enrings the barky fingers of the elm.

O, how I love thee! how I dote on thee!

A Midsummer Night's Dream

To gild refined gold, to paint the lily,

To throw a perfume on the violet,

. . . .

Is wasteful and ridiculous excess.

King John

. . .Before the sun rose he was harness'd light,

And to the field goes he; where every flower

Did, as a prophet, weep what it foresaw

In Hector's wrath.

Troilus and Cressida

Since brass, nor stone, nor earth, nor boundless sea,

But sad mortality o'ersways their power,

How with this rage shall beauty hold a plea,

Whose action is no stronger than a flower?

Sonnet 65

Here's flowers for you:

Hot lavender, mints, savory, marjoram . . .

The Winter's Tale

O! How much more doth beauty beauteous seem

By that sweet ornament which truth doth give!

The rose looks fair, but fairer we it deem

For that sweet odour which doth in it live.

Sonnet 54

Why, he was met even now

As mad as the vexed sea, singing aloud,

Crowned with rank fumiter and furrow-weeds,

With hardocks, hemlock, nettles, cuckooflowers,

Darnel, and all the idle weeds that grow

In our sustaining corn.

King Lear

Hail, many-colour'd messenger, that ne'er

Dost disobey the wife of Jupiter;

Who with thy saffron wings upon my flowers

Diffusest honey-drops, refreshing showers . . .

The Tempest

Sir, the year growing ancient,

Not yet on summer's death nor on the birth

Of trembling winter, the fairest flowers o' th' season

Are our carnations and streak'd gillyvors . . .

The Winter's Tale

The summer's flower is to the summer sweet,

Though to itself it only live and die,

But if that flower with base infection meet,

The basest weed outbraves his dignity:

For sweetest things turn sourest by their deeds;

Lilies that fester smell far worse than weeds.

Sonnet 94

For thou art pleasant, gamesome, passing courteous,

But slow in speech, yet sweet as spring-time flowers.

The Taming of the Shrew

The forward violet thus did I chide

Sweet thief, whence didst thou steal thy sweet that smells,

If not from my love's breath? The purple pride

Which on thy soft cheek for complexion dwells

In my love's veins thou hast too grossly dy'd.

Sonnet 99

Fair ladies masked, are roses in their bud.

Dismasked, their damask sweet commixture shown,

Are angels vailing clouds, or roses blown.

Love's Labour's Lost

Where the bee sucks, there suck I:

In a cowslip's bell I lie . . .

The Tempest

There's rosemary, that's for remembrance.

Pray you, love, remember.

Hamlet

I must have saffron, to colour the warden pies.

The Winter's Tale

Now stand you on the top of happy hours,

And many maiden gardens, yet unset,

With virtuous wish would bear you living flowers

Much liker than your painted counterfeit . . .

Sonnet 16

Nor did I wonder at the lily's white,

Nor praise the deep vermillion in the rose . . .

Sonnet 99

It standeth north-north-east and by east

from the west corner of thy curious-knotted garden.

There did I see that low-spirited swain . . .

Love's Labour's Lost

To lie that way thou go'st, not whence thou comest:

Suppose the singing birds musicians,

The grass whereon thou tread'st the presence strew'd,

The flowers fair ladies, and thy steps no more

Than a delightful measure or a dance . . .

Richard II

And, most dear actors,

eat no onions nor garlic,

for we are to utter sweet breath . . .

A Midsummer Night's Dream

The marigold, that goes to bed wi' th' sun

And with him rises, weeping: these are the flowers

Of middle summer . . .

The Winter's Tale

Nay, by my faith,

I think you are more beholding to the night

than to fern seed for your walking invisible.

Henry IV Part I

What art thou fall'n? What subtle hole is this,

Whose mouth is cover'd with rude-growing briers,

Upon whose leaves are drops of new-shed blood

As fresh as morning dew distill'd on flowers?

Titus Andronicus

. . . bold oxlips and

The crown imperial; lilies of all kinds,

The flower-de-luce being one! O, these I lack,

To make you garlands of, and my sweet friend,

To strew him o'er and o'er!

The Winter's Tale

. . . But flowers distill'd, though they with winter meet,

Leese but their show; their substance still lives sweet.

Sonnet 5

This bud of love, by summer's ripening breath,

May prove a beauteous flower when next we meet.

Good night, good night! as sweet repose and rest

Come to thy heart as that within my breast!

Romeo and Juliet

And both like serpents are, who though they feed

On sweetest flowers, yet they poison breed.

Pericles, Prince of Tyre

For she did his hairy temples then had rounded

With a coronet of fresh and fragrant flowers.

A Midsummer Night's Dream

With fairest flowers

While summer lasts, and I live here, Fidele,

I'll sweeten thy sad grave . . .

Cymbeline

Away before me to sweet beds of flow'rs;

Love-thoughts lie rich when canopied with bow'rs.

Twelfth Night

But she perforce withholds the lovèd boy,

Crowns him with flowers, and makes him all her joy.

A Midsummer Night's Dream

When daisies pied and violets blue,

And lady-smocks all silver-white,

And cuckoo-buds of yellow hue

Do paint the meadows with delight,

The cuckoo then on every tree

Mocks married men . . .

Love's Labour's Lost

He came with flowers to strew his lady's grave;

And bid me stand aloof, and so I did . . .

Romeo and Juliet

He hath a garden circummured with brick,

Whose western side is with a vineyard back'd;

And to that vineyard is a planched gate,

That makes his opening with this bigger key:

This other doth command a little door

Which from the vineyard to the garden leads;

There have I made my promise

Upon the heavy middle of the night

To call upon him.

Measure for Measure

Heigh-ho, sing, heigh-ho, unto the green holly.

Most friendship is feigning, most loving mere folly.

Then, heigh-ho, the holly

This life is most jolly.

As You Like It

Let one attend him with a silver basin

Full of rose-water and bestrewed with flowers . . .

The Taming of the Shrew

Fairies use flowers for their charactery.

A Midsummer Night's Dream

Should not in this best garden of the world,
Our fertile France, put up her lovely visage?

Henry V

Behold our patroness, the life of Rome!

Call all your tribes together, praise the gods,

And make triumphant fires; strew flowers before them

Unshout the noise that banish'd Marcius,

Repeal him with the welcome of his mother;

Cry 'Welcome, ladies, welcome!'

Coriolanus

Look like th' innocent flower,

But be the serpent under't.

Macbeth

. . . We will with some strange pastime solace them,

Such as the shortness of the time can shape;

For revels, dances, masks and merry hours

Forerun fair Love, strewing her way with flowers.

Love's Labour's Lost

What's in a name? That which we call a rose,

By any other name would smell as sweet.

Romeo and Juliet

With sun and moon, with earth and sea's rich gems,

With April's first-born flowers, and all things rare

That heaven's air in this huge rondure hems . . .

Sonnet 21

The flowers are sweet, their colours fresh and trim,

But true beauty liv'd and died with him.

Venus and Adonis

What sport shall we devise here in this garden

To drive away the heavy thought of care?

Richard II

As there is no true cuckold but calamity, so beauty's a flower.

Twelfth Night

On a day, alack the day!

Love, whose month was ever May,

Spied a blossom passing fair,

Playing in the wanton air. . .

Sonnets to Sundry Notes of Music II

I know a bank where the wild thyme blows,

Where oxlips and the nodding violet grows,

Quite overcanopied with luscious woodbine,

With sweet musk-roses, and with eglantine.

A Midsummer Night's Dream

I will go root away

The noisome weeds, which without profit suck

The soil's fertility from wholesome flowers.

Richard II

Fair flowers that are not gather'd in their prime

Rot, and consume themselves in little time.

Venus and Adonis

*I*ndex to Plants

Note that, while each of these plants is either mentioned in one of Shakespeare's plays, poems, or sonnets or is commonly grown in Shakespeare gardens, improved cultivars may be pictured.

Page 4   Rose (*Rosa* 'Fruhlingsgold')

Page 12   Love-in-idleness, heartsease, pansy (*Viola tricolor*)

Pages 13–14   Love-in-idleness, heartsease, pansy (*Viola tricolor* 'Helen Mount')

Page 17   Columbine (*Aquilegia* 'Spring Song')

Pages 18–19   Columbine (*Aquilegia* McKana Giant series)

Page 21   Cottage garden with peonies (*Paeonia* spp.), cranesbill (*Geranium* spp.), and pinks (*Dianthus* spp.)

Page 23   Daffodil (*Narcissus* 'Fortissimo')

Pages 24–25   Daffodil (*Narcissus* 'Actaea')

Page 27   Monkshood, aconitum (*Aconitum carmichaelii* 'Arendsii')

Page 29   Poppy (*Papaver orientale* 'Turkish Delight')

Pages 30–31   Poppy (*Papaver orientale*)

Page 33   Woodbine (*Lonicera periclymenum* 'Serotina')

Page 35   Madonna lily (*Lilium candidum*)

Page 37   Pincushion flower (*Scabiosa* 'Pink Mist')

Page 39   Checkered lily, snakeshead (*Fritillaria meleagris*)

Page 41   English lavender (*Lavandula angustifolia* 'Munstead')

Pages 42–43   English lavender (*Lavandula angustifolia* 'Hidcote')

Page 45   Cabbage rose (*Rosa centifolia*)

Pages 46–47   Rose (*Rosa* 'Rose de Rescht')

Page 49   Cuckooflower (*Cardamine pratensis*)

Page 51   Lilac sage (*Salvia verticillata* 'Purple Rain')

Pages 52–53   Bluebell, wild hyacinth (*Hyacinthoides nonscriptus*)

Page 55   Carnation (*Dianthus* 'Rose Monica Wyatt')

Page 57   Tiger lily (*Lilium tigrinum*)

Page 59   Checkered lily, snakeshead (*Fritillaria meleagris* 'Alba')

Pages 60–61   English garden with tulips (*Tulipa* 'Blue Heron')

Page 63   Sweet violet (*Viola odorata* 'Coeur d'Alsace')

Pages 64–65   Sweet violet (*Viola odorata*)

Page 67   Damask rose (*Rosa damascena*)

Pages 68–69   Gallica rose (*Rosa* 'Charles de Mills')

Page 71   Cowslip (*Primula veris*)

Page 73   Rosemary (*Rosmarinus officinalis* 'Gorizia')

Page 75   Saffron crocus (*Crocus sativus*)

Page 77   Daisy (*Bellis perennis* 'Margery Fish')

Page 79   Gallica rose (*Rosa* 'Cardinal de Richelieu')

Pages 80–81   Gallica rose (*Rosa gallica* var. *officinalis*)

Page 83   Rose walk

Pages 84–85   English knot garden

Page 87   Pink (*Dianthus* sp.)

Page 89   Bride's onion (*Allium neapolitanum*)

Page 91   Pot marigold, calendula (*Calendula officinalis* 'Indian Prince')

Page 93   Fern (*Dryopteris* sp.)

Page 95   Snakeroot, flat-leaved eryngium (*Eryngium planum* 'Blaukappe')

Page 97   Crown imperial (*Fritillaria imperialis*)

Page 98–99   Crown imperial (*Fritillaria imperialis*)

Page 101   Nectaroscordum (*Nectaroscordum siculum* ssp. *bulgaricum*)

Page 103   Rose (*Rosa* 'Simplicity')

Page 105   Yellow flag (*Iris pseudacorus*)

Page 107   Dwarf iris (*Iris reticulata*)

Page 109   Borage (*Borago officinalis*)

Pages 110–111   Borage (*Borago officinalis*)

Page 113   Yarrow (*Achillea* sp.)

Page 115   Dead nettle (*Lamium* 'Beedham's White')

Page 117   Foxglove (*Digitalis purpurea* 'Excelsior Mix')

Page 119   Daisy (*Bellis perennis*) with star-of-Persia (*Allium christophii*)

Page 121   Masterwort (*Astrantia* sp.)

Page 123   Walled garden with peonies (*Paeonia* sp.)

Pages 124–125   Peonies (*Paeonia* 'West Elkton')

Page 127   Holly (*Ilex aquifolium*)

Page 129   Star-of-Bethlehem (*Ornithogalum umbellatum*)

Page 131   Solitary clematis, crowfoot (*Clematis integrifolia*)

Pages 132–133   Clemtis (*Clematis* 'Nelly Moser')

Page 135   The Shakespeare Garden at Varangeville Sur Mer, France

Page 137   Container of thyme (*Thymus* spp.)

Page 139   Cupid's dart (*Catananche caerulea*)

Page 141   Cushion spurge (*Euphorbia polychroma*)

Pages 142–143   Cottage garden with purple-leaf sand cherry (*Prunus* x *cistenus*), roses (*Rosa* 'Betty Prior'), peonies (*Paeonia* sp.), and lamb's ears (*Stachys byzantina*)

Page 145   Lungwort (*Pulmonaria saccharata*)

Page 147   Rose (*Rosa* 'Gold Medal')

Page 149   Sweet pea (*Lathyrus odoratus*)

Pages 150–151   Blue wild indigo (*Baptisia australis*)

Page 153   Globeflower (*Trollius* sp.)

Page 155   Cottage garden

Page 157   Aster (*Aster novae-angliae*)

Pages 158–159   Aster (*Aster novae-angliae*)

Page 161   Buttercup (*Ranunculus* sp.)

Page 163   Eglantine, sweetbrier (*Rosa eglanteria*)

Pages 164–165   Rose (*Rosa moyesii*)

Page 167   Cranesbill (*Geranium* 'Johnson's Blue')

Pages 168–169   Cranesbill (*Geranium sanguineum* var. *striatum* 'Splendens')

Page 171   Tulip (*Tulipa* 'Lilac Wonder')

Pages 172–173   Cottage garden with lupines (*Lupinus* spp.), foxgloves (*Digitalis* spp.), and delphiniums (*Delphinium* spp.)

Index to Works Quoted

As You Like It, 126

Coriolanus, 138

Cymbeline, 112

Hamlet, 16, 72

Henry IV Part I, 92

Henry IV Part II, 26

Henry V, 134

King John, 34

King Lear, 48

Love's Labour's Lost, 66, 82, 118, 144

Macbeth, 140

Measure for Measure, 122

A Midsummer Night's Dream. 12, 32, 88, 108, 116, 130, 162

Othello, 20, 28

Pericles, Prince of Tyre, 104

Richard II, 86, 154, 166

Romeo and Juliet, 102, 120, 146

Sonnet 5, 100

Sonnet 16, 76

Sonnet 21, 148

Sonnet 54, 44

Sonnet 65, 38

Sonnet 94, 56

Sonnet 99, 62, 78

Sonnets to Sundry Notes of Music II, 160

The Taming of the Shrew, 58, 128

The Tempest, 50, 70

Titus Andronicus, 94

Troilus and Cressida, 36

Twelfth Night, 114, 156

Venus and Adonis, 152, 170

The Winter's Tale, 22, 40, 54, 74, 90, 96

Places to Visit

Museums and Libraries

Folger Shakespeare Library
201 East Capitol Street, S.E.
Washington, D.C. 20003-1094

The Shakespeare Birthplace Trust
The Shakespeare Center
Henley St., Stratford-upon-Avon
Warwickshire CV37 6QW England

Gardens

Colorado Shakespeare Garden
Boulder, Colorado

Garden of Shakespeare's Flowers
Golden Gate Park
San Francisco, California

Shakespeare Garden
Bethel Public Library
Bethel, Connecticut

Shakespeare Garden
Brooklyn Botanic Garden
Brooklyn, New York

Shakespeare Garden
Burlington, Iowa

Shakespeare Garden
Cedarbrook Park
Plainfield, New Jersey

Shakespeare Garden
Central Park at 79th Street
New York, New York

Shakespeare Garden
College of St. Elizabeth
Convent Station, New Jersey

Shakespeare Garden
The Cultural Gardens
Cleveland, Ohio

Shakespeare Garden
Ellis Park
Cedar Rapids, Iowa

Shakespeare Garden
The Huntington Library,
Art Collections and
Botanical Gardens
1151 Oxford Road
San Marino, CA 91108

The Shakespeare Gardens
Huron and Ontario Streets
Stratford, Ontario

Shakespeare Garden
Lincoln Park
Chicago. Illinois

Shakespeare Garden
Northwestern University
Evanston, Illinois

Shakespeare Garden
St. Norbert College
De Pere, Wisconsin

Shakespeare Garden
Stanley Park
Vancouver, British Columbia

The Shakespeare Garden
University of South Dakota
Vermillion, South Dakota

Shakespeare Garden
The University of the South
Sewanee, Tennessee

Shakespeare Garden
University of Tennessee
at Chattanooga
Chattanooga, Tennessee

Shakespeare Garden
Vassar College
Poughkeepsie, New York

Shakespeare Garden
The Wichita Gardens
Wichita, Kansas

Shakespeare Gardens
and Anne Hathaway Cottage
Wessington Springs, South Dakota

Shakespeare Garden
Wynton M. Blount Cultural Park
Montgomery, Alabama

A FRIEDMAN/FAIRFAX BOOK
Please visit our website: www.metrobooks.com
© 2001 by Michael Friedman Publishing Group, Inc.

Library of Congress Cataloging-in-Publication Data

Shakespeare, William, 1564-1616.
[Selections, 2000]
Shakespeare's flowers / introduction by Frances Owens.
p. cm.
Includes index.
ISBN 1-58663-125-X (alk. paper)
1. Shakespeare, William, 1564-1616—Quotations. 2. Flowers—Quotations, maxims, etc.

3. Plants—Quotations, maxims, etc. 4. Quotations, English. I. Title.

PR2892 .2000
828'.302—dc21
00-049450

Editor: Susan Lauzau
Art Director: Jeff Batzli
Designer: Midori Nakamura
Photo Editor: Kate Perry
Production Manager: Richela Fabian Morgan

Color separations by Fine Arts Repro House Co., Ltd
Printed in Hong Kong by Midas Printing Limited

1 3 5 7 9 10 8 6 4 2

Distributed by Sterling Publishing Company, Inc.
387 Park Avenue South
New York, NY 10016
Distributed in Canada by Sterling Publishing
Canadian Manda Group
One Atlantic Avenue, Suite 105
Toronto, Ontario, Canada M6K 3E7
Distributed in Australia by
Capricorn Link (Australia) Pty Ltd.
P.O. Box 6651
Baulkham Hills, Business Centre, NSW 2153, Australia

Photo Credits

©Rob Cardillo: 37, 87

©David Cavagnaro: 64–65, 171

©R. Todd Davis: 59, 158–159

©Dembinsky Photo Associates: 14–15

©Brian Durell: 51, 57, 141, 147, 157

©Elizabeth Whiting & Associates: 109, 123

Garden Picture Library: 21, 33, 39, 41, 46–47, 49, 63, 67, 71, 75, 77, 80–81, 89, 93, 106–107, 127, 129, 139, 150–151, 168–169, 172–173

©Marge Garfield: 45

©John Glover: 29, 35, 52–53, 55, 60–61, 68–69, 83, 84–85, 137, 155

©Lisa Hollender: 4

©Dency Kane: 1, 2, 27, 73, 79, 91, 95, 105, 115, 117, 119, 121, 124–125, 131, 142–143, 145, 163, 167

©Krischan Photography: 18–19, 103

©Charles Mann: 153

©Clive Nichols: 13, 30–31, 42–43, 98–99, 101, 135, 149

©Jerry Pavia: 110–111, 164–165

©Cheryl Richter: 17, 23, 24–25, 97, 113, 132–133, 161, endpapers